PARTY FUN

From the editors of
OWL and *Chickadee Magazines*

Edited by Catherine Ripley

OWL

Greey de Pencier Books

Books from OWL are published in Canada by Greey de Pencier Books, 56 The Esplanade, Suite 306, Toronto, Ontario, M5E 1A7.

* OWL, the OWL character and the OWL colophon are trademarks of the Young Naturalist Foundation. Greey de Pencier Books is a licensed user of trademarks of the Young Naturalist Foundation.

Canadian Cataloguing in Publication Data

Main entry under title:

Party fun

ISBN 0–920775–41–1

1. Children's parties — Juvenile literature.
I. Ripley, Catherine, 1957–

GV1205.P37 1989   j793.2'1   C89–093357–X

Special thanks to Sylvia Funston, editor of OWL Magazine, and Janis Nostbakken, editor of Chickadee Magazine, and to all those people who worked with them on creating most of the ideas and images found in this book: Marilyn Baillie, Lina Di Nardo, Laima Dingwall, Lynn Harvey, Nancy Harvey, Elizabeth MacLeod, Jonathan Milne, Nick Milton, Laurie Peters, Cathy Ripley, Wycliffe Smith, Lyn Thomas, Linda Weissinger and Valerie Wyatt.

The publishers would also like to thank Green Tiger Press for permission to use an idea based on the book Hanimals by Mario Mariotti.

Design Director: Wycliffe Smith

Designer: Julie Colantonio

Photography: Ray Boudreau (Cover, pages 4–5, 7, 8–9, 11, 12–13, 14–15, 16, 20–21, 22–23, 24–25, 26–27, 31), Matthew Levin (pages 18–19), Tony Thomas (page 29).

Illustration: Julie Colantonio (pages 7, 8–10, 32), Dan Hobbs, (pages 28–29), Vesna Krstanovich (pages 17, 30).

Printed in Hong Kong

Contents

Getting Ready

Fun and Games

Gifts to Make

Come On Over!

Make some stamps to decorate your own party invitations and thank-you notes. While you're at it, design some great gift wrap and some placemats too. Ready? Set? Stamp!

You'll Need:

Thick string
Scissors
White glue
Small milk cartons
Flat dishes or pans
Poster or powdered paint
Plain paper (*Typing or construction paper work well for cards. Grocery bags or tissue wrapping paper work well for gift wrap. Use thicker paper for placemats.*)
Newspaper

Here's How:

■ Using the white glue, draw a shape or write a word on the bottom of each milk carton.

■ REMEMBER: If you want to print a word, you'll have to write it backwards. To check your spelling, hold the stamp up to a mirror.

■ Cut a length of string long enough to fit the shape or word and press it down into the glue.

■ Let your stamps dry completely. This may take several hours.

■ Spread out newspaper on a flat surface.

■ Pour a thin layer of paint into a dish and fold the paper for your invitations. Line them up in a row on top of the newspaper.

■ Put your stamp into the paint and press down.

■ Lift the stamp up to see if all of the string has absorbed paint. When it has, let the excess paint drip off into the pan.

■ Do a few practice stamps on the newspaper before stamping the designs on your party invitations.

Getting Ready

How much string do you have in your house?

Probably not as much as Francis Johnson of Minnesota. In 28 years he collected enough string to make a ball that weighed as much as two elephants and was as big as a small car!

No-Bake Cake

Here's a delicious cake that you "bake" in the freezer! Make it a day ahead of party time.

You'll Need:

24 chocolate chip cookies
175 mL (³/₄ cup) uncooked oatmeal
125 mL (¹/₂ cup) melted butter
2 L (¹/₂ gallon) ice cream (*You can use two different flavors if you like.*)
1 plastic bag
Rolling pin
Bowl
Forks, spoons and a knife
24 cm (9¹/₂ inch) springform pan
Decorations (*Try using grapes, berries, almonds, chocolate chips, colored sprinkles, smarties, jelly beans and other candies.*)

Here's How:

■ Put the ice cream in the fridge to soften slightly while you complete the following steps.
■ Put 16 cookies in a plastic bag and crush them well with the rolling pin.
■ Put the crushed cookies in a bowl and add 125 mL (¹/₂ cup) oatmeal.
■ Add 75 mL (¹/₄ cup) melted butter and stir.
■ Press this mixture evenly into the bottom of the pan.
■ Scoop out half the ice cream and smooth down on top of the crust with a metal spoon.
■ Now crush the rest of the cookies in the bag and mix with the remaining oatmeal and butter in a bowl.

■ Spread this mixture over the ice cream, and then add the rest of the ice cream to the pan.
■ Decorate the cake any way you like.
■ Freeze overnight. Before serving, run a knife around the edge of the pan and then remove the sides.
■ This cake serves about 12 people.

The biggest birthday party of all . . .

According to a Chinese tradition, everybody's birthday is celebrated on the Chinese New Year's Day along with the start of a new year.

Getting Ready

Hats On

Create high party spirits with these fabulous and funny hats.
And who will hit the party piñata?

PARTY PIÑATA

Make this great game a couple of days ahead of time, and you'll be ready to celebrate the Latin American way.

You'll Need:

Large balloon (*Blow it up, tie the end and tape the end to a table.*)
Paste (*Mix 250 mL (1 cup) flour with 500 mL (2 cups) water in a bowl.*)
Newspaper sheets, cut into strips
Tape
Several long pieces of string
Decorating materials
Treats (wrapped candies, peanuts, raisin boxes . . .)
Blindfold
Baseball bat or stick

Here's How:

■ Spread a few newspaper sheets around the balloon to keep the table clean.
■ Dip the newspaper strips into the paste one by one.
■ Run your fingers down each strip to remove any extra paste.
■ Start wrapping the strips around the balloon, leaving an empty space at the neck about 8 cm (3 inches) in diameter.
■ First put on a layer of strips that go up and down.
■ Then put on a layer of strips that go around the balloon.

Tape ▶

■ Let the piñata dry for three days and then pop the balloon.
■ Decorate the piñata and put the treats inside through the hole.
■ Now tape the ends of each piece of string inside the hole.

■ Reinforce each piece with tape several times, and then hang the piñata at eye level. Make sure there is lots of clear space around it.
■ When it's time to play the piñata game, give the first player a blindfold and the bat.
■ Make sure that everyone is standing well away from the player and the piñata, and then tell your friend to take three swings at the piñata. Then it is the next player's turn.
■ When the piñata breaks, everyone has a chance to scoop up the scattered treats.

SUPER HATS

Use this simple pattern and add odds and ends from around the house to make funny party hats.

You'll Need:

Newspaper sheets
Scissors
Glue or tape
Decorating materials (*Use cotton puffs, paper chains, material scraps and whatever else you can think of.*)

Getting Ready

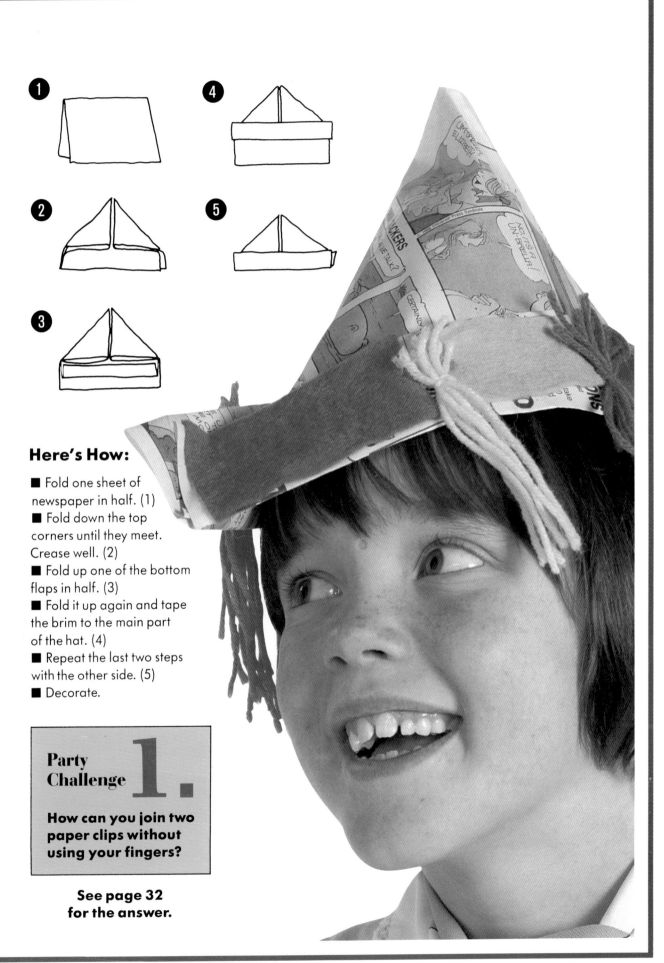

Here's How:

■ Fold one sheet of newspaper in half. (1)

■ Fold down the top corners until they meet. Crease well. (2)

■ Fold up one of the bottom flaps in half. (3)

■ Fold it up again and tape the brim to the main part of the hat. (4)

■ Repeat the last two steps with the other side. (5)

■ Decorate.

Party Challenge 1.

How can you join two paper clips without using your fingers?

See page 32 for the answer.

Party Loot

Give your friends some tiny gifts to take home.
Everyone likes party loot!

DRESS-UP DISGUISE

Hook an egg-carton-cup nose onto a pair of toy glasses with pipe cleaners. Add a paper mustache if you like.

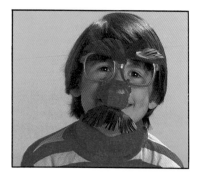

BATHTUB BOAT

Secure a toothpick mast in a styrofoam egg-carton cup or walnut half with plasticene. Poke on a sail made out of construction paper, and set sail for bathtubs unknown!

CREEPY CRAWLIES

Turn pebbles or stones into creepy-crawly creatures by decorating them with markers or paints. Tape on pipe cleaners for legs, feelers or wings.

Lucky Guests

A *potlatch* is a Northwest Coast Indian celebration often given to honor a person taking a new place in the village ranks. The word *potlatch* is a Chinook word meaning "to give." Today, children at a *potlatch* are given some money and candies, while grown-ups can receive blankets, towels, clothing and money. But long ago, shield-shaped sheets of beaten copper, blankets and even canoes were given away. Now that's a lot of loot!

LOOT BAGS

Make each guest a special loot bag to save their goodies in. If you like, your guests can decorate them when they arrive.

You'll Need:

Small paper bags
Scissors
White glue
Crayons or markers
Decorations (*Colored paper, tinfoil, pipe cleaners and cupcake liners all work well.*)

Here's How:

■ Fold over the top third of the paper bag.
■ Cut the corners off the folded flap and make a rounded nose.
■ Decorate the bag to look like any animal you want.

Getting Ready

Let's Decorate!

Add these great "surprise" decorations to the placemats created with your stamps, and your party will sparkle.

RIDDLE JARS

Decorate the party table with a riddle jar for each guest.

You'll Need:

Small clean jars (*Baby food jars work well.*)
Construction paper
White glue
Decorating materials (wool, sparkles, fabric scraps, paper cutouts)
Scissors
Colored markers and pencils
Treats
Riddles

Here's How:

■ Trace around the top of the jar twice on some paper.
■ Cut out each circle. Trim one circle so it fits snugly inside the lid.

■ On the bigger circle, print the riddle question. Print the answer on the smaller circle.
■ Glue the question circle to the top of the lid and then glue the answer circle to the inside. Let dry.
■ Decorate the jar, fill it with treats and put the lid on.
■ Repeat these steps until you have a jar for each guest.

BALLOON BUST

Burst balloons to discover where hidden treasure lies.

You'll Need:

Hiding places
Treats for all your guests
Paper and pencil
Scissors
Balloons
A few pins

Here's How:

■ Write a sentence describing where you have hidden the treats in your house. Leave plenty of space between the words.

Getting Ready

■ Cut the sentence up, leaving one word on each piece of paper.
■ Before you blow up each balloon, mark it with an X and then stuff one piece of paper into it.

■ When it's time to search for the hidden treasure, tell your guests to find and burst all the balloons marked with an X. (Don't hang them up too high!)
■ To find the treasure, they must put the words of the sentence in the proper order.

Party Challenge 2.

How can you make it impossible for a friend to lift up his or her ring finger?

See page 32 for the answer.

Giggle Games

How easily do you get the giggles? These party games are sure to get you started!

WHERE, OH WHERE, IS THE WONDERWART?

Pay attention, now. This is a very serious game . . . no laughing allowed!

You'll Need:

3 or more friends
Space large enough for your guests to sit in a circle

Here's How:

■ Tell your guests that when their turns come, they must turn to the person on their left and say, "Friend, this is serious. Where, oh where, is the wonderwart?"

■ The whole group then places their right hands over their eyebrows, turns right, left and right again, saying "Where, oh where, is the wonderwart?"

■ The person who has just been spoken to now turns to the person on his or her left, and so on.

■ The winner is the person who can keep a straight face the longest. No smirks, no smiles, no laughs allowed.

STARE DARE

Dare a friend to stare at you without laughing. Whoever laughs first is out, and another player steps up to challenge the winner.

Fun and Games

Feeling Low?

Put on a smile no matter how rotten you feel, and believe it or not, you may actually start to feel better. Some scientists believe that the movements your face muscles make when you smile send messages to your brain that make you feel happy. Try it!

ANIMAL NOISES

Ask your friends to sit in a circle while one blindfolded player stands in the middle. Give this player a long cardboard tube and spin him or her three times. The blindfolded player then gently taps someone in the circle. The person who has been tapped must make an animal noise. If the blindfolded player guesses who made the noise, they exchange places and the noisemaker is now "it." If not, spin the blindfolded player again and so on.

TONGUE TWISTERS

Who can say these phrases ten times fast?
- Toy boat
- Seven sleepy sheep
- Pink pig
- Rubber baby buggy bumpers

CHUCKLE BELLY

How long can you hold in the chuckles?

You'll Need:

Large area to spread out in Friends (the more, the merrier!)

Here's How:

- Ask one person to lie flat on his or her back.
- The second person puts his or her head on the first person's tummy.
- The other guests lie down in the same way, heads on each others' tummies, and wait for the chuckles to begin.

SWIMMING CHICKENS?

This is a crazy verison of "Simon Says." The leader calls out an animal action such as "Ducks fly!" Then he or she acts it out, and the guests follow suit. The leader calls out a second action, acts it out, and so on.
BUT . . . once in a while the leader calls out a mixed-up animal action such as "Chickens swim!" Anyone who follows the leader and acts out the mix-up loses and must take over as leader.

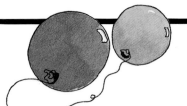

Party Favorites

Try the memory game, pass the parcel and bounce a balloon . . . everyone will want to play!

PASS THE PARCEL

Who will find the small present inside the big package?

You'll Need:

Small prize
Small piece of gift wrap
Various containers ranging from
    small to large
Paper (plain brown paper,
    newspaper or gift wrap)
String
Tape
Scissors
Music

Here's How:

■ Wrap the prize in gift wrap.
■ Place the wrapped prize inside a bigger box and wrap it.
■ Continue wrapping in this manner until you have a large parcel to pass around a circle of guests.
■ Adding string can make the unwrapping tough . . . and fun!

■ The players sit in a circle. When the music starts, they pass the parcel from person to person. When the music stops, the player who has the parcel quickly starts to unwrap it. When the music starts again, the player must give up and pass it on.
■ The player who unwraps the prize can keep it!

Fun and Games

MEMORY TRAY

"Hmmmmmm . . . what was that skinny thing beside the apple? It was a . . . a . . . a shoelace. That's it!"
Play this game and find out how good *your* memory is.

You'll Need:

Tray
10-20 household objects
Pencils and paper (enough for
    your guests)
A watch

Here's How:

■ Before the party begins, arrange the objects on the tray. The older the guests, the more objects you can include.
■ Ask everyone to sit in a circle, and then put the tray in the middle.

■ Tell everyone they have one minute to look at the objects on the tray. Then they will be asked to write down (or draw, if they can't write) all the objects they can remember.
■ Keep an eye on your watch. When a minute is up, remove the tray and let your guests go to work. Whoever can remember the most objects wins the game.

Party Challenge 3.

How can you stick a pin into a balloon without bursting it?

See page 32 for the answer.

BALLOON BOUNCING

Set up a race course. Give each guest a blown-up balloon and tell them they must "bounce" the balloon across the finish line. Easy, right? Then tell them that they're not allowed to use their hands or let the balloon touch the ground!

Spider Web!

This spider game is great fun, even if you don't like spiders.

SEED SPIDERS

Turn pumpkin seeds into spiders and play ''Stick the Spider on the Web.''

You'll Need:

Clean, dry pumpkin seeds (*Use cardboard ovals if seeds are unavailable.*)
Markers or poster paints
Woolen legs (*Cut thumb-length pieces from different colored balls of wool. You'll need 4 short strands for each guest, plus some extras.*)
Yarn or string
Scissors
White glue
Web design on large piece of bristol board or cardboard
Masking tape
Blindfold

Here's How:

■ Before your guests arrive, create the bodies of the seed spiders.

■ Tie 4 legs together with a longer piece of yarn or string.
■ Glue the seed body and woolen legs together. Let dry.

■ Tape the spider-web design on a wall.
■ When the guests arrive invite them to decorate a spider for themselves.
■ Then stick a loop of masking tape on the bottom of each guest's spider.
■ Have each guest take 5 giant steps away from the web.
■ Blindfold the first player and spin him or her several times.
■ Then ask the player to ''Stick the Spider on the Web!''
■ Whoever puts his or her spider closest to the center wins the game.

Which is stronger, spider silk or steel?

Spider silk can be stronger than steel of the same thickness! It is also extremely versatile. Most spiders use it to spin webs. The amazing diving spider weaves a silken room underwater. Then it carries down bubbles of air to fill the room, and there it lives.

Handy Animals

Turn your hands into fabulous creatures by making these extraordinary hand puppets.

WOOLY PUPPETS

How many different creatures can you and your friends make?

You'll Need:

Old gloves or mittens (*Collect one for each guest.*)
Decorating materials (pipe cleaners, sparkles, construction paper . . .)
White glue in several dishes
Cotton swabs
Scissors

Here's How:

■ Put the decorating materials in the center of the table.
■ Lay a glove or mitten in front of each chair and invite your guests to sit down.
■ Give each guest a cotton swab to dip into the glue and let them start decorating.
■ When the puppets are finished, perform a party song!

Thumbs Up for Thumbs!

Thumbs are terrific! Without them, you'd find it difficult to do many things such as turning a door knob, or even holding this book. You don't believe it? Tape your thumbs to the sides of your hands and try living without them!

Fun and Games

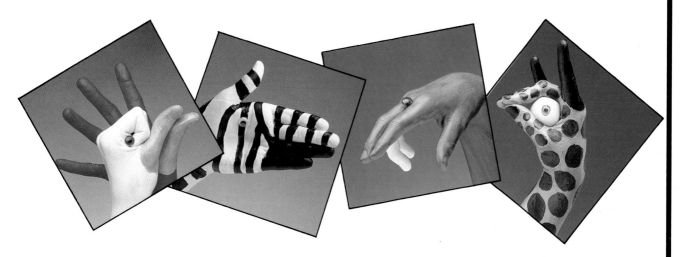

ANIMAL PUPPETS

Discover the animals waiting at your fingertips. All you need is some paint and imagination.

You'll Need:

Newspaper
Water-based poster paints
Baby oil
Paintbrushes
Dishes
Soap and water (to wash your
    hand afterwards)

Here's How:

■ Spread out newspaper on a large table and set up enough chairs for your guests.
■ Pour paint into the dishes and add a few drops of baby oil to each.
■ Then let your friends go wild with their paintbrushes!

V.I.P. Gifts

Grown-ups are V.I.P.s (Very Important People)...right? Your parents, grandparents, aunts or uncles deserve the very best, and what could be better than a picture of you?

BAKE A PHOTO

After you take these photos out of the oven and let them cool, they can be hung up.

You'll Need:

Photo frame dough (*Mix 575 mL (2¼ cups) flour, 250 mL (1 cup) salt and 250 mL (1 cup) water together in a bowl.*)
Rolling pin
Glass
2-8 photos, depending on size (*Small photos work best.*)
Fork
Straw
Cookie sheet
Paints or markers
Ribbon or wool
Oven preheated to 150°C (300°F)

Party Challenge 4.

How can you pick up an ice cube without using your fingers?

See page 32 for the answer.

Here's How:

■ Knead the dough. When it is smooth, roll it out on a well-floured surface until it's the consistency of thick pie crust.
■ Use the glass to cut out dough circles and place them on a cookie sheet.
■ After trimming the photos so that they are smaller than the circles, center each one on top of a dough circle.
■ Fold the dough edges over the photos and press them gently with a fork.
■ Poke a hole through the top of each photo frame with the straw.
■ Bake for an hour or until the dough is hard.
■ When the photo frames have cooled, decorate them and thread ribbons through the holes at the top.

Gifts to Make

PORTRAIT PAPERWEIGHT

Most V.I.P.s need help keeping their papers in order, so give them a paperweight.

You'll Need:

Photo of you (*A dried flower or a homemade picture also works well.*)
Clean, small jar with lid
Salt
Colored chalks
Metal strainer
Newspaper
White glue
Stir stick

Here's How:

■ Put the photo, face down, in the bottom of the jar.
■ Pour a handful of salt onto a folded piece of newspaper. (1)
■ Hold the strainer over the salt. Now rub the chalk through the mesh and onto the salt. (2)
■ Stir the chalk and salt together until evenly mixed.
■ Now use the newspaper to pour part of the mixture into the jar.
■ Start again, but this time, use a different color of chalk or plain salt, so you can build up pretty layers in the jar. (3)

■ When the jar is full, gently shake it to remove any air pockets and add a little more salt.
■ Line the inside edge of the lid with white glue. (4)
■ Tightly screw the lid in place and turn the jar over. Now your face beams out from on top!

Easy Pizazz

**These little extras are easy to make, and fun to give any time.
Jazz up a special friend!**

JAZZY JEWELRY

**String some paper
beads and make a hit!**

You'll Need:

Old color magazines
(*Ask an adult if you
can cut them up.*)
    Pencil
    Scissors
    White glue
    Yarn
    Safety pin

Here's How:

■ Cut long triangles out of the
magazine pages. The base of
each triangle should measure
about 5 cm (2 inches). (1)

■ Squeeze a line of white glue
down one side of the triangle. (2)

■ Start at the wide end of the
triangle and roll it tightly around
a pencil. (3)

■ When the glue is dry, pull the
pencil out.

■ String the beads on yarn end-
to-end to make a bracelet or
necklace. (4)

■ For an ''Egyptian'' effect,
ask an adult to use a needle and
thread to string the beads side-
by-side. To make a brooch, ask
an adult to push a safety pin
through the back of a bead.

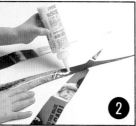

Gifts to Make

FANCY LACES

Decorate plain, white shoelaces with colored markers, and your friends can have the fanciest feet on the block. Don't forget to make some for yourself!

NOODLE NECKLACE

To make a nifty necklace, collect pasta pieces of all shapes and sizes. Color them with markers and string them on brightly colored yarn.

Living Jewelry

Believe it or not, thousands of years ago Greek women made musical barrettes by stringing cicada bugs in their hair on golden threads.

Super Stuffers

Quarters and dimes,
Scissors and string!
Where can you put
All of these things?
Inside these two easy-to-make containers, of course!

OINK BANK

Turn a plain, old bleach bottle into a piggy bank with class.

You'll Need:

Clean bleach bottle with cap
Corks or empty spools
Construction paper
Felt
Pipe cleaners
Scissors
White glue

Here's How:

■ Lay the bottle on its side and ask an adult to help you cut a slit big enough for coins to fit through.
■ On the opposite side, cut two holes big enough for the cork or spools to slide into for feet. Be sure the holes are set far enough apart to let the bank stand upright.
■ Use the cap as the pig's nose, and use the paper, felt and pipe cleaners to make ears, eyes and a tail.
■ Oink, Oink!

PATCHWORK PENCIL HOLDERS

Collect some empty cans and fabric scraps. Then start patching!

You'll Need:

Empty cans
Fabric scraps
White paper
Tape
Scissors
White glue

Here's How:

■ Cover each can with a piece of white paper. Tape to secure.
■ Cut the fabric into squares, circles or any shapes you like.
■ Glue the scraps onto the cans to make a patchwork design.

Is a pig a pig?

No, it isn't. Unlike other animals such as dogs and cats, a pig will not overeat. It knows exactly when it's had enough and stops before it's stuffed!

Gifts to Make

Just for the Fun of It!

Here are some games to make and give away. But they're so much fun, you may want to keep them yourself.

TWO-IN-ONE GAME

Turn one cardboard box into two great games. Then try out your tossing skills!

You'll Need:

Large cardboard box
Scissors
Rolled-up pair of old socks
Paint

Markers
Clothespegs or ice cream sticks
3 rings (*Cut rings from yogurt container lids or use rubber canning rings.*)
Paper and pencil

Gifts to Make

Here's How:

■ On one side of the box paint a face, and after it has dried, cut out a big, wide mouth.

■ On the other side, paint 9 widely-spaced dots and number them. Poke clothespegs or ice cream sticks through each dot.

■ Put the rings into the box along with the socks.

■ Write out these instructions on a card:

Sock Toss: Can you toss the socks through the mouth? Each time you do, take a step backward. How far can you step back and still throw the socks into the mouth?

Ring Toss: Stand back and toss the rings at the clothespegs or ice cream sticks. When a ring lands on a peg, add the number of the peg to your score.

CHALLENGE CUP

How long will it take to get a "cup in one?"

You'll Need:

Ruler

38 cm (15 inches) of string

Paper drinking cup (*Decorate to make the gift extra special.*)

Tape

Paper and pencil

Here's How:

■ Turn the cup upside down and poke a small hole through the bottom.

■ Thread the string through the hole and knot securely.

■ Tie the other end of the string to the end of the ruler and tape in place.

■ Write out these instructions on a card:

Hold the ruler in one hand. How many times in a row can you get the cup to land on top of the ruler?

Party Challenge 5.

How can you turn yourself into a mindreader?

See page 32 for the answer.

Pet Presents

If you and your friends love pets, share some party fun with them too!

KITTEN CRAZES

Give your kitten a set of balls made out of crumpled newspaper or construction paper. To make the balls especially appealing, rub catnip on them! Kittens love to chase these paper balls. They also love to pounce on rope "snakes." To make a snake, simply cut off a *thick* piece of nylon twine. (Avoid using long pieces of string, thread or elastic for this game.)

HAMSTER HIDEAWAYS

Make some hideaway tunnels for your hamster out of empty cardboard tubes. Decorate them with non-toxic markers and place them in the hamster cage. Hamsters like hiding in them … they may even sleep in them and chew on them too!

Which pets have been around the longest?

Dogs were probably the first wild animals to become tame pets. Their ancestors, wolflike animals, came close to campfires for tidbits, and eventually people kept the friendliest ones around permanently. While dogs have lived around people as long as 12,000 years, cats have been around for about 4,000 years, and goldfish have been bred for over 1,000. That's some history!

DOGGONE DOG BONES

Your hound will gobble these snacks up lickety-split.

You'll Need:

375 mL (1 1/2 cup) whole wheat flour, 125 mL (1/2 cup) grated cheese, 50 mL (1/4 cup) bacon fat, 125 mL (1/2 cup) water and 15 mL (1 tbsp) soya sauce (*Mix together well.*)
Greased cookie sheet
Bowl
Fork
Oven preheated to 200° C (400° F)

Here's How:

■ Mould small pieces of dough into bone shapes. The "bones" should be no more than 1 cm (1/2 inch) thick.
■ Place on the cookie sheet.
■ Bake for 30 minutes.
■When cool, store in a paper bag.

Gifts to Make

WARNING:
Don't give these
biscuits to dogs
with heart disease
or those on
low-sodium diets.
The biscuits are
high in salt.

Answers

Party Challenge 1.

Fold one long strip of paper into thirds as shown below. Join the first two sections with a paper clip, then the second two sections with another paper clip. Stand well away from other people and pull hard on both ends of the paper. Ta da!

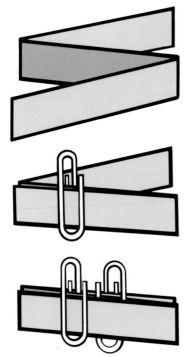

Party Challenge 2.

Ask a friend to place his or her hand on a table, palm down with fingers spread out. Now ask your friend to tuck the middle finger under. Can he or she lift the ring finger?

Party Challenge 3.

Blow up a balloon three-quarters full and knot it. Make a cross out of clear tape on the balloon. Now push a straight pin through the center of the tape cross! WARNING: Hold onto the balloon and pin tightly, and be sure to pull out the pin before putting the balloon down.

Party Challenge 4.

All you need in addition to the ice cube is some salt and a piece of string. Lay the end of a wet piece of string on top of the ice cube. Sprinkle some salt on top and wait about one minute. Then lift.

Party Challenge 5.

You need to plan this "mind-reading" trick with a friend in advance. You leave the room while your friend and the others stay in the room and decide upon an object. When you return, you have to guess what the object is. You do not speak. (You're too busy "concentrating" on the image in everyone's minds!) Your friend asks you if various objects in the room are the right ones. The question about the correct item always comes after your friend asks about a *black* object.